# OVERCOMING
## THE STORMS OF
# LIFE

## FINDING STRENGTH IN ADVERSITY

### Paye V. Bagnon

Scripture references in this book are taken from the Authorized King James Version (KJV) except otherwise stated.

www.WorldwidePublishingGroup.com
7710-T Cherry Park Dr, Ste 224
Houston, Texas 77095
(713) 766-4271

ISBN:

# Acknowledgements

This book is aided by the Holy Spirit, whose anointing on my life and ministry has propelled me into undertaking this task. To put it bluntly, the Holy Spirit gave me the grace and the ability to carry out this assignment.

I acknowledge my children, Paye & Paynell Bagnon, and all those who aided me in the course of my life and ministry. I am truly grateful for your support and all the tireless and sleepless nights you spent encouraging me. May God richly reward your labor of love abundantly. I know that you too may be going through difficult storms in your life, but I assure you that God has not forgotten about you and will surely see you through.

May God, whom you honor with your faith and service, reward you most abundantly.

PAYE V. BAGNON

# Foreword

In the middle of life's storms, we often find ourselves lost, searching for ways to weather the storms that assail us. During these tumultuous moments, we may wonder if we are truly alone in our struggles. In *Overcoming The Storms of Life*, Pastor Paye Bagnon provides a practical and holistic approach to facing life's challenges head-on.

The author, writing from personal experience, has provided us with a comprehensive toolkit for building resilience and coping with life's adversities. He artfully weaves physical, psychological, and spiritual approaches to help you overcome your various storms as conquerors. Understanding how storms serve as catalysts for personal growth and stronger connections with the Lord and others will breathe new life into every struggle.

As you read the book, you will be immersed in a journey of faith and empowerment. You will find solace in the fact that you are not alone in your trials. You will be reminded of and strengthened by the revelation that God truly cares for you, and you are never alone in your storms. And that the Holy Spirit is your Helper from heaven!

The truths within these pages can transform your perspective on life's trials. They remind you that you are loved and cherished, and hope remains alive no matter how daunting the challenges may seem. Each chapter is enriched with valuable insights rooted in biblical references that will inspire and guide you toward the brighter, more fulfilling future God has planned for you.

I urge you to embrace Pastor Bagnon's teachings with an open heart and mind. You will discover within these pages the secrets to conquering the storms of life and emerging stronger and more resilient than ever before. Let the wisdom they convey enter your heart and mind and build your faith to experience healing, restoration, and ultimate triumph.

*Overcoming the Storms of Life* is truly an answer to prayer. May you reap the full benefits of a book written with you and your needs in mind.

**Bishop Darlingston G. Johnson**
Presiding Bishop,
*Harvest Intercontinental Ministries Unlimited*

# Preface

This book provides a practical approach to overcoming life's storms. It allows you to develop resilience and coping skills during life's storms using physical, psychological, and spiritual approaches.

In this world of difficulties and challenging experiences, we often wonder where our lives are heading and what next steps we should take. In the pages of this book, you will discover that there are reasons why life's storms occur.

Storms create opportunities for us to deepen our relationship, walk with God, and also help us support and comfort one another during tough times. God sends storms into our lives to get our attention, mature us, build us up, and bring us to a place of strength where His glory shines brighter.

To get through the storms in your life, you need to know the following:

1. Who you are in Christ
2. What Jesus has done for you at Calvary
3. The resurrection power
4. The work of the Holy Spirit in your life

What Jesus is doing on your behalf right now at the right hand of the Father. Hebrews 7:25 says that He's making daily intercession for you.

Everyone goes through various storms, but our comfort is that we have an anchor in Christ. Therefore, we are encouraged never to give up or lose hope when faced with adversity.

This book is about helping the reader brace themselves and receive encouragement about overcoming the storms of life.

# CONTENTS

PAYE V. BAGNON

# Introduction

You are not alone! This is the greatest truth that should flood your mind. As you read this book, let this truth become a living reality in your life and your watchword.

It doesn't matter what the circumstances or feelings; get that truth circulating in your mind. Everything you need to find peace, strength, and victory is found in that truth. You are not alone because God is with you, and countless people worldwide are experiencing the same challenges you are facing right now.

These challenges usually come with feelings of frustration, destitution, and hopelessness. Many people, including you, may feel like giving up, quitting, or just walking away. For many, it may feel like hope is gone, and life has become one big disappointment or a nightmarish abysmal failure.

Why? The answer is simple; as people live, they are going through life, and at certain times life can be a difficult road to navigate.

Navigating marital problems, financial difficulties, poor health, physical or spiritual issues, and all the vicissitudes of life's disappointments can become a very tall order. While going through turbulent times, people feel abandoned, isolated, and insecure.

A sense of loneliness, helplessness, and inner groaning of desolation overtakes the mind and consciousness at such moments, leaving you feeling like no one cares and that you are all alone. But the truth is someone really cares.

You might not realize it now. You might not even see it when you need it most. It might even be difficult to understand or comprehend, and everything inside of you is screaming that no one possibly cares. But someone does—someone cares. And that someone cares for you immensely.

As you continue reading through the pages of this book, you will realize that you are loved and that apart from God, you matter to somebody somewhere.

As you peruse this book, you will find that God can and desires with an intense longing to serve as a solution to whatever you are experiencing. This book contains Bible references that will inspire, motivate, impact, and lead you to your destiny.

As a result, don't just read this book with your eyes. Read it with your heart and mind, and prepare yourself for recovery, reinstatement, deliverance, and breakthrough.

Conquering The Storms of Life is a teaching tool that, if applied from within, will equip you to overpower the storms of your life.

# Chapter 1

# Embracing The Tempest

## Understanding Life's Trials and God's Purpose

According to the American Heritage Dictionary of the English Language, a storm is a violent agitation of human society, a civil, political, or domestic commotion, or a violent outbreak.

A storm can also be characterized as a mental ruckus that affects the psychological health of an individual when faced with situations that become bleak and unmanageable.

Whenever a person faces this type of mental collision, it affects their physical and spiritual life in countless negative ways, creating a spiral effect of downward living. These negative spiraling events can come upon any individual at any time from many different sources—they are bred from different situations, obstacles, problems, circumstances, and difficulties.

Although it may appear all these mechanisms were designed to destroy you, hinder you, and stop you, you and I have the awesome power to overcome these life traps and propel our thinking into victorious, positive, and far-reaching realities. The truth is that no situation has come upon a person, now, in the past, or will in the future, that they can't overcome.

As such, it doesn't matter how your storms come, whether they are violent agitations from society, whether they are rooted in a mental commotion, or they are spiritual. As a child of God, you already know how it will end—in your favor. Therefore, prepare yourself right now to obtain victory as an overcomer.

### Why Do Storms Come?

As mentioned above, every person experiences a storm or storms in their life. To track the reasons why storms come, we must first identify the source of the storms. Is the storm coming from God, or is it coming from Satan? Strangely, whether from God or Satan, you may feel the same impact.

You may feel like it doesn't matter where the storm originated. If that is your thinking, you are wrong because the motivation behind the storm is different depending on its source.

If we consider God the source of the storm, we can safely say that these tumultuous situations bring us closer to God. The motivation of the storm originating from God is to draw you closer to Him.

I know that is not what you want to hear, and you might even disagree with me right now. As you read that statement, I can even hear thoughts going through your mind. You might ask yourself, "How and why would a loving God use a storm to draw me closer to Him? Doesn't He have better ways of getting my attention? Why should I suffer and experience pain and/or turmoil just for God to grab my attention?"

Although our knowledge is limited as to why, the truth is that He can, and sometimes He does allow storms in our lives. But He also chooses and does choose to help us even with the storms He has allowed.

Before you read on, I want you to know that just because you are experiencing a storm doesn't mean God hates you or is mad at you. Of course, it does not by any stretch of the imagination mean He doesn't love you anymore or is punishing you.

The fact that you are experiencing a storm means the complete opposite. It signifies that God loves you more than you think. He loves you enough to grab your attention. This is because that is what storms do. They grab our attention and refocus our thinking on God's goodness, faithfulness, and commitment to our cause of life. Storms are catalysts for a mental shift—refocusing you in the right direction.

---

*Just because you are experiencing a storm*
*doesn't mean that God hates you or is mad at you.*

---

That notion is far from the truth since we may consider Satan the source of all storms. However, when Satan is the originator, we are fully aware of his motivation in stirring up the storm. The scriptures declare he is a murderer from the beginning: *"You belong to your father, the devil, and you want to carry out your father's desire. He was a murderer from the beginning, not holding to the truth, for there is no truth in him. When he lies, he speaks his native language, for he is a liar and the father of lies"* (John 8:44 NIV).

He is a tormentor, a deceiver, a trickster, and a hater of humanity. When he unleashes a storm against you, he is determined to deter and keep you from being all God wants you to be.

His intention in unleashing a storm against you is to stop you, embarrass you, and make you quit. He doesn't want you to have what God has ordained for your life, and he uses the storm to pull you away from God.

That has been his agenda all along. His motivation is fueled by hatred to make you a failure in life. But you must know you can overcome any storm regardless of its origin. Oh yes, you have what it takes to do it.

You have the overpowering, overcoming ability in Christ Jesus to do just that. However, in our own strength, we lack the resources and abilities to take on life's challenges headlong. But God helps us in times of need.

The Scripture says, *"God is our refuge and strength, a very present help in trouble. Therefore, will we not fear, though the Earth be removed, and though the mountains be carried into the midst of the sea; Though the waters thereof roar and be troubled, though the mountains shake with the swelling thereof. Selah"* (Psalms 46:1-3).

Know the source of your storm. If it comes from God, it is meant to draw you closer, so embrace it and allow the process to work in you as you are pulled into His purpose, reconstructed for your assignment, and repositioned for destiny work and kingdom living.

If it is from Satan, know that you are in a battle. Still, God is also aware of it and will never leave you comfortless; instead, He will give you the strength and ability to come out as a winner.

---

*Know the source of your storm.*
*If it is coming from God, it is meant to draw you closer,*
*so embrace it and allow the process to work in you*
*as you are pulled into His purpose.*

---

### Lessons from the Darkness

Our sufferings are never a surprise to the Lord. He knows what we are going through. And even when the storms originate from the camp of satanic powers, God has a way of circumventing the evil purposes of the storm and using it for His glory and our benefit.

*"And we know that all things work together for good to those who love God, to those who are the called according to His purpose"* (Romans 8:28).

When we train our minds to reflect on God's divine purpose as we face our hardships, He will, in turn, help us to respond to our trials and negativities in a God-honoring way. How we enter the storm tremendously affects how we progress and come out of it. Let's consider the Lord and seek to understand His purposes, ways, and reasons behind our cloudy days.

There are four lessons we can learn when facing our storms. Considering these lessons, we can find meaning and purpose in life, even in our dark moments.

*1. Hardship is Cleansing*

In our self-absorbed world, our flesh has become the dominant force of mental authority. Therefore, developing selfish attitudes, mixed-up priorities, and ungodly habits is easy. The pressures that come upon us from stormy situations are meant to bring the impurities of our unhealthy lifestyles to the forefront to redirect us to a place of repentance.

Therefore, our trials are intended to purify us and guide us back to God in godliness, humility, gentleness, and kindness, but never intended to ruin our lives.

*2. We are Meant to Help Others*

Another purpose of difficulties is to prepare our hearts to be more compassionate and kinder to other people's situations. Ordinarily, we tend to concentrate on ourselves, but God wants us to comfort others.

Whatever God has made us to be is never intended solely for personal consumption. It is meant to go around to reach a world that does not recognize or acknowledge Him.

The Lord uses our challenges to equip us to serve others. As we experience suffering, we will learn about God's sufficiency, comforting presence, and strength to help us endure.

---

*The Lord uses our challenges*
*to equip us to serve others.*

---

It is observed that testimonies of those who went through times of difficulty are always authentic and more helpful to others who are also experiencing some difficulties in their own lives. Those to whom we minister will recognize that we not only acknowledge their pain but also understand it.

Our pains add credibility to our victory and assure the next person that our advice can be trusted. *"Who comforts us in all our tribulation, that we may be able to comfort those who are in any trouble, with the comfort with which we ourselves are comforted by God"* (2 Corinthians 1:4).

### 3. God Promises Victory

We face storms so we may experience the power and promises of God. He has declared that He will be there when we pass through the fire. There is never a time when God desires to leave you to handle your challenging situations all by yourself. He will always make a way of escape for you because He is your hope.

*"When you pass through the waters, I will be with you; And through the rivers, they shall not overflow you. When you walk through the fire, you shall not be burned, Nor shall the flame scorch you. For I am the Lord your God, The Holy One of Israel, your Savior..."* (Isaiah 43:2-3)

Isn't it good news to know that God promises to provide a path through any trial we face? The answer is, yes! When the disciples of Jesus were faced with a physical storm while on the sea, they probably wondered how long the storm would last and whether they would make it safely to shore, but yes, they all made it to shore alive because Jesus calmed the storm.

Most likely, they wished the storm had never happened. The Scriptures vividly stated that the storm was so tumultuous that it pounded the ship with a strong wind to the magnitude that it filled the traveling vessel with water. But had they somehow avoided this storm, they would have missed the opportunity of the demonstration of Jesus' power over the sea and wind.

*"But He was in the stern, asleep on a pillow. And they awoke Him and said to Him, "Teacher, do You not care that we are perishing?" Then He arose and rebuked the wind, and said to the sea, "Peace, be still!" And the wind ceased and there was a great calm. But He said to them, "Why are you so fearful? How is it that you have no faith?" And they feared exceedingly and said to one another, "Who can this be, that even the wind and the sea obey Him!" (Mark 4:38-41).*

The frightening situation was transformed into a revelation of the Savior's divine nature. God wants to make His power known through our trials.

---

*God promises to provide a path*
*through every trial we face.*

---

### 4. God is Ever-Present

One of the most important things to learn about the storms in our lives is the revelatory truth of the continual presence of God. He has promised, "I will never leave you or forsake you," and yes, He is a promise keeper who always shows up amid our storms. The truth is that God is always with us, especially during a storm.

The most important thing He gives us in our experiences of storms is an awareness of His presence. He is always there! At first, the disciples became more afraid, knowing that Jesus was not there with them in that terrifying storm. Even after Jesus showed up, their fears increased because they thought He was a ghost.

But as they recognized His presence in power, their fear turned to relief and hope. Similarly, even though we may not sense God's presence during a crisis, He has promised to always be with us.

*"But the boat was now in the middle of the sea, tossed by the waves, for the wind was contrary. Now in the fourth watch of the night, Jesus went to them, walking on the sea. And when the disciples saw Him walking on the sea, they were troubled, saying, "It is a ghost!" And they cried out for fear. But immediately, Jesus spoke to them, saying, "Be of good cheer! It is I; do not be afraid"* (Matthew 14:24-27).

The assurance that the Lord will never leave us provides immediate comfort, an infusion of courage, and a sense of confidence to endure. No one enjoys suffering. But in the hands of the Almighty God, our trials become tools for His purpose in our lives.

God uses hardship to shape believers into the people He intends them to be. Jesus allowed the disciples to experience the fear and anxiety of being in a boat on a raging sea. He permitted them to suffer because He had something far more important to teach them. He wanted the disciples to recognize their helplessness. Then they would see His sufficiency and realize how much they need Him to survive.

Ask God to reveal His abiding presence during your troubles. And remember that He will always provide for your spiritual needs to help you both endure and grow stronger in your Christian faith.

### *Sources of Storms*

It has already been established in this book that storms can come from Satan or God. However, there is also another source of our storms which comes from our association with others since storms can also be created by our own mistakes and wrong decisions that we have made on Earth. Be aware that the devil is not the originator of all the storms of life. Some storms can result from God permitting the devil to test you.

The story of Job is a good example here. In Job Chapter 1, the Bible says that the Lord asked Satan, "Where have you come from?" Satan replied, "I go to and fro the earth," the Lord asked Satan, "Have you considered my servant Job?"

Satan then goes on to explain to the Lord that Job is serving God because he has been blessed by Him in everything concerning his life. Then Satan suggests to God that if the hedge of protection that secures Job's life and blessings is removed, and he, Satan, is allowed to attack him, he will certainly curse God.

As a result, the Lord removed the hedge around Job with a clear and concise instruction not to hurt or harm his life. Every time there is a satanic intrusion into your affairs by the permission of God, the Lord is doing so to help keep you on track or deepen your relationship with Him.

The most important thing to keep in mind and secure in your heart is the uncontestable truth that you will make it through that storm. No matter what happens, you will make it through your storm! When you see yourself as an overcomer, the storms of life will never break you; instead, they shall make you! Consider these points:

1. Storms of life do not come to disconnect you from your destiny; instead, they reconnect you to destiny.
2. Storms of life are meant to re-align you to your destiny.
3. Storms are not meant to destroy you, but they are meant to empower you.
4. Storms merely reveal to you how God's Word is ready to heal.

---

*When you see yourself as an overcomer, the storms of life will not break you, but instead, they shall make you.*

---

### You are a Conqueror

A conqueror is someone who gains an exceptional triumph. This person is completely victorious and understands that each victory is a constant reminder that they are a winner and will continue to win.

Your storms will tell you that you are a failure, a loser, and you are defeated. But that's definitely a lie from the pit of hell! Rather, you are a winner because you already have the power to conquer your storms, and that makes you a "conqueror."

*"Who shall separate us from the love of God? Shall tribulation, shall trial, shall persecution, shall famine, shall nakedness, or shall spear or sword? It is written that for your sake, we are killed all day long, and we are counted as sheep for the slaughter" (Romans 8:35-37).*

The above declaration of Paul reminds us that in every situation and every problem, God has empowered us to overcome. It may be a storm in your marriage, workplace, relationships, or even ministry. It may come with spiritual torment, obstacles, and problems. Still, you should know within yourself that you have the power to overcome it. The affirmation is that in all things, we are more than conquerors through Him who loves us.

There is a greater one in us that helps us to overcome the world. This is the absolute confidence that children of God have. Jesus is in you and has become the hope of your glory.

Jesus in you is greater than Satan, who is around you, trying to attack and frustrate you. Develop the confidence to remind Satan through the power of rebuke that He has no place of authority in your life because there is a greater one who commands your life.

*"You are of God, little children, and have overcome them because He who is in you is greater than he who is in the world"* (1 John 4:4).

*Develop the confidence to remind
Satan, through the power of rebuke that he
has no place of authority in your life.*

You can do all things through Christ. Nothing is lacking or kept back from you. You have access to power, strength, and ability that comes from God. Jesus strengthens you to succeed and overcome. He empowers you to become a conqueror. Amid the circumstances, conditions, and problems that have kept you down, you have the dominating power of the Most High God working in you. And this power can be accessed through the Word of God.

During the problem, the Word of God dominates and trumps every secondary force, including the forces of darkness. You are in Christ, and He is in you. His love for you has guaranteed your victory through what He did on the cross of Calvary.

Everything that was designed to hold you back from living in the fullness of the greatness of our God was left in the grave because He resurrected you from your problems. The Holy Spirit is assigned to keep you living in resurrection power daily. He comes to maintain your reconnection to the promises of God.

Make daily confessions that God is with you and believe in that confession. There's power in it because Jesus is making daily intercessions for you before the Father. There is no other person who can pray for you who is better than Jesus, and there is no other person who is closer to you than the Holy Spirit. Trust Jesus, the Holy Spirit, and God's plans will see you through to victory.

No matter whom you request prayers from, you will still go through the storms of life. However, always be reminded of the fact that

God is able to deliver you from any storm. Jesus is at the right hand of God, making intercessions for you.

Whatever battles you are currently facing does not mean God has abandoned you or thrown you away. He cares about your life. He cares about the things you are going through. He understands, and He has made a way of escape for you.

It doesn't matter what you are facing, whether it is a child gone astray, a broken marriage, demonic attacks from your background, or mental disturbances fueled by fear. Know that you are more than a conqueror through Him who loves you. You have been loved by the Lord, and through Jesus Christ, you are a conqueror.

---

*God cares about your life. He cares about the things you are going through. He understands, and He has made a way of escape for you.*

---

Once you understand that you are a conqueror, you must maintain that level of truth in your mind. You accomplish this by building your house, your life, your thoughts, your actions, and your faith in the Word of God.

Every life that is built on God's Words is rooted in Jesus Christ. This gives us a level of security unmatched in this world because whoever is rooted in Jesus Christ can receive no harm from the devil. There is nothing the enemy can do to you.

However, if winds come, let them. If storms come, let them. If floods come, let them. Whatever inferior power that has decided to fight against you doesn't matter. What matters is that you are rooted in Christ; therefore, they will encounter the power of the greater

One in you. That encounter will always ensure your victory because He who is in you has the greatest power of all.

# Chapter 2

# Embracing Reverence

## The Journey to Deepening Your Relationship with God

Those who fear and do the work of God will stand forever. Those who ignore the Word of God will surely fail. If you decide now to obey God and be rooted in His Word, you will achieve peace in the middle of you storm. The more dominance the Word of God plays in your life, the more overcoming power you have.

When the prophet Isaiah told King Hezekiah that he should set his house in order because he was going to die, Hezekiah turned around and petitioned the Lord saying, "Lord you know this one thing, you know how I have worked with you so dearly. But I want you to know, God; this cannot be the final truth" (2 Kings 20:1-11; Isaiah 38:1-8).

In whatever situation, always be reminded that God is faithful. So, the Lord turned Hezekiah's situation around by calling upon Him in time of need. He can turn yours around as well.

### Become a Doer of God's Word

Build yourself and your spirit on the Word of God. The key to conquering or overcoming the storms of life is doing the will of God. God's Word should be a major responsive force and tool to combat every satanic attack. In Matthew 4:1-6 the Bible states that Jesus Christ was hungry for 40 days and 40 nights.

The Holy Spirit led him into the wilderness to be tested by the devil, and the encounter was fierce. However, Jesus responded to the devil in proportion to the Word of God, and Satan could do nothing but bow to it. Every storm is parallel to the Word of God.

If anyone hears the Word and becomes a doer of the Word, their storms will automatically be calmed. You will be able to live above principalities and powers and be free from torment because God will grant you peace. You can either be wise enough to be a doer of God's Word or be ready to become a doer of God's Word. Either of these will propel you into dominion over your storms.

### There's Power in the Word

The Word of God is a counterattack to every satanic attack that comes against you. The Word of God gives you strength, boldness, and the ability to pray with power. If you want to overcome and conquer your storms, you must learn that there is power in God's Word and become a doer of it. Don't receive it partially or improperly but resolve to study the Word of God diligently in order to be *"A workman who is not ashamed but rightly dividing the Word of truth"* (2 Timothy 2:15).

People who have heard the Word of God but do not apply it to their lives have a minimal impact against satanic attacks which come upon them. You must yield to the Word of God. When you do not yield to the Word of God, the attacks against you will be harder to win. Victory is in the power of the Word of God.

When we study the Word of God, it is not just to get more information; Jesus tells us that we learn more to do more. In other words, there should be a corresponding action as you hear the Word of God. God's Word builds faith and does not lead you into jeopardy. God's Word will not allow you to fall asleep in the middle of your storm. The Word of God will counterattack the wind and the storm that have come against your life.

---

*The Word of God is a counterattack*
*to every satanic attack that comes against you.*

---

### Rest in the Word

The Bible contains many passages that offer hope, encouragement, and wisdom to help us navigate difficult times. This is why so many people turn to the Word of God during their difficulties. They do so in search of comfort, guidance, and strength within its pages. One of the most well-known passages in this regard is probably Psalm 23, which speaks of God's presence and protection even amid darkness and danger.

Other passages that offer comfort and hope include Isaiah 41:10, which says, *"Fear not, for I am with you; be not dismayed, for I am your God; I will strengthen you, I will help you, I will uphold you with my righteous right hand,"* and Matthew 11:28, which says, *"Come to me, all you who are weary and burdened, and I will give you rest."*

The Scriptures encourage us to trust God's wisdom and guidance rather than relying on our understanding. When we focus on God's ability rather than our own, we are already making the steps toward becoming victorious.

*"Trust in the Lord with all your heart and lean not on your understanding; in all your ways submit to him, and he will make your paths straight"* (Proverbs 3:5-6).

### Trust the Word during Adversity

In this fallen world, adversity is a part of life, and there will be times when we face challenges that test our strength and resilience. The Word of God encourages us to not give up or give in when things get tough. It empowers us to draw on our inner reserves of strength and determination to overcome those obstacles before us.

In times of crisis, it's important to stay focused on our goals and to keep moving forward, even if the progress is slow. We can take comfort in knowing that our strength comes not just from our efforts but from the support of others and our faith in Jesus Christ.

The Word of God constantly reminds us that we are capable of overcoming adversity and that we should not let difficult circumstances defeat us. By staying strong in the Word and persevering through life's challenges, we can emerge stronger and more resilient than before.

By turning to the Bible and seeking its wisdom, we can find the strength to face whatever challenges come our way. Even when we face loss and hardship, we can continue to trust in God's goodness and faithfulness. We can worship God amidst our pain, recognizing that God is still worthy of our praise even when things are difficult.

*By staying strong in the Word and persevering through life's challenges, you can emerge stronger and more resilient than ever before.*

PAYE V. BAGNON

# Chapter 3

# Faith Tested

## Navigating Life's Storms with Unwavering Trust

While on a journey across the sea, the disciples of Jesus encountered a physical storm. The storm created much fear in the disciples' hearts. Note that fear is an enemy to man and will always cripple you from walking in the authority of Jesus Christ.

Amidst the roaring waves and rocking boats, these chosen few failed to recall the lessons they learned from Jesus himself. They failed to know His purpose and His power. Even after witnessing the awesome feat of their master Jesus walking on the water directly toward them, it couldn't bring them immediate relief. Still, instead, it increased their fear (Matthew 14:26).

In our strength, we lack sufficient resources and the ability to meet life's challenges. However, God consistently provides what we need. Therefore, when trouble comes, it's not the time to forget about God or struggle to recall past answers to prayer or how the Holy Spirit guided us in times past. On the contrary, it is the time to run to God, seek Him, and submit to His all-sufficient ability to help us in time of need.

Don't allow your present situation to be the only reality or allow your mind to spin with future negative implications. Remind yourself of past victories to strengthen your resolve to defeat the enemy.

Also, rebuke every troubled emotion that inhibits clear thinking. God loves you, and He is always there for you—always!

On one occasion, Jesus realizing that His disciples were operating with little faith, rebuked their faithlessness. After witnessing the mighty power of Jesus in rebuking the wind and the sea, they confessed with amazement, saying to one another, *"Who can this man be, that even the winds and sea obey Him"* (Matthew 8:23-27).

Paul teaches the church in Rome that faith comes by hearing the Word of God. In the most disastrous, difficult times and very complex situations, Jesus asks us, His sons and daughters, "Where is your faith?" We must develop an ear to hear the Word of God for our faith to grow.

When the disciples faced that storm on the ship, Jesus was asleep on the same ship during the same storm. He was not bothered by the storm, nor was he bothered when the disciples woke Him up. Rather, He rebuked the storm, and it became calm.

It is important to understand that storms will never stop raging against us. They will never stop coming or advancing in our lives. As one storm is rebuked from hurting us, another storm will begin, but what will help us through the storm is the Word of God.

Jesus said to His disciples, "Where is your faith?" In other words, Jesus told them you already have faith to overcome and destroy this storm, so why didn't you use it? That is a fact! No storm will overtake your life because Jesus has developed your faith enough to conquer your storms, so your faith at each moment should make you stronger amid your storms.

### Use Your Faith

The Disciples had the ability to use their faith to repel, destroy and/or rebuke the storm, but they allowed fear to dominate them. Fear is a formidable opposition to your faith, and it comes to keep you in the storms of life, which faith should liberate you from. When fear rises, faith must get up to quell it.

Whenever there is an open door of fear, you should empower your faith to get up, and then fear will go out. Faith responds to the confidence you have in the Word of God, and the power of faith is actualized in your ability to speak the Word of God in any given situation.

---

*Every time there is an open door of fear,*
*you should empower your faith to get up,*
*and then fear will go out.*

---

When you become a doer of the Word, then your faith will never disappoint you, and fear will disappear from your life. However, when your faith is paralyzed, demons dominate you and lead you into something that is not right or holy. When your faith is paralyzed, the Word of God cannot be strong in you, and things don't work the way they should. But when you believe what God says and stand on it, then automatically, fear cannot have a foothold in your life.

### *Do Not Paralyze Your Faith*

No matter how big your Goliath is, how tumultuous that storm is, or how rocky your journey might be, go ahead and exercise your faith by putting the Word of God into action through confession. Speak the Word of God, and life will spring from within to halt death trying to take control of you.

It is time for you to speak to your problems, speak to your circumstances, choose to believe the Word of God, and not doubt it. Whatever you have been through or are going through, you can dominate, conquer, and destroy it.

Jesus said to his disciples, *"Because of your unbelief; for assuredly, I say to you, if you have faith as a mustard seed, you will say to this mountain, 'Move from here to there,' and it will move; and nothing will be impossible for you"* (Matthew 17:20).

### *Count It All Joy And Be Joyful*

In all things, be joyful. This might sound like a cliché, but it's not. One thing a storm hates is having a positive attitude amid it. James, the brother of Jesus and Bishop of the Church, encourages us to count it all joy when we fall into problems, temptations, and hardships.

It's easy to worry about your life when things are bad and not going how you expect them to. Worry is a sign of fear. Trials and tribulations come to discourage you and dampen your attitude, making you sad, depressed, and deflated. When the enemy has successfully driven you to the place of mental disarray, then he can easily win the battle because your consciousness has already been defeated.

*"My brethren, count it all joy when you fall into various trials, knowing that the testing of your faith produces patience. But let patience have its perfect work, that you may be perfect and complete, lacking nothing"* (James 1:3-4).

What do you think it means to count it all joy? The answer is quite simple. It means to become joyful. Whenever you encounter various kinds of difficulties, temptations, marital setbacks, or life situations, please don't allow them to take your joy, change your attitude, or warp your disposition. But in all things, give thanks because this is the will of God in Christ Jesus concerning you. Counter your attacks with the joy of the Lord.

### *Keep Praise On Your Lips And Joy In Your Heart*

Don't you know that the joy of the Lord is your strength? You can be easily conquered without strength, but with strength, you can fight and fight to win. With the strength of the Lord, you will be undefeated.

What happens when you lose your joy? What happens when you lose your strength? What happens when you are without strength? What happens if you cannot overcome or conquer that adversity? What happens when you've just lost something so precious to you? What happens when the storms of life break you up and throw you off balance? The Bible says we should rejoice, be happy and move on. Why? It is because God is with you.

Paul encourages us to rejoice in the Lord always (Philippians 4:4). You might be saying to yourself that Paul was an apostle, full of power and anointing, so it is easy for Him to say that. However, Paul wrote these words while he was in prison. Yes, prison! Imagine someone being chained, heavily guarded, and enduring tremendous pain, yet he says to rejoice in the Lord.

When you learn to rejoice in the Lord, you train your eyes to see the goodness of the Lord in your life, even in the most unlikely circumstances. Do not lose heart but rejoice and watch the storms lose their grip over your life.

---

*Keep praise on your lips and joy in your heart...*
*do not lose heart but rejoice and watch the storms*
*lose their grip over your life.*

---

### Be Steadfast

Develop the ability to see far ahead. If you only focus on what is in front of you, you will never see what is beyond you. Storms have a funny way of keeping your view very narrow. But when you broaden your vision, you will begin to see things about the storms in your life that are working for your benefit. This is what the storm doesn't want you to see, but God does want you to see. James 1:3-4 exhorts us that on the other side of our storms, great things are happening for our benefit, such as:

1. Storms produce patience
2. Storms come to perfect us
3. Storms come to make us whole
4. Storms come so that we would lack nothing.

So how do we gain these benefits? It is by being steadfast. Developing an attitude of steadfastness will help you see beyond your current situation and focus your eyes on the result. The middle of a storm is not the time to let go of your vision and allow your problems to hold you down.

God wants your faithfulness to show up, especially while going through a storm, and you can accomplish this by developing an attitude of steadfastness. *"I would have lost heart unless I had believed that I would have seen the goodness of the Lord"* (Psalms 27:13).

You must be steadfast in reading the Word of God and putting it into practice. The more dominant God's Word is in you, the more you forge ahead in overcoming the storms of life. James continues to encourage the believers to become doers, not just hearers of the Word of God.

Going through a storm will require the Word of God to take you through the storm. No challenge comes without a promise in the Word. Just learn to align yourself and your faith with the Word of God, applying it in every situation, and the glory will show up and give you victorious results.

Find Scriptures connected to what you are facing, and meditate on them continually, allowing the Scripture to become a part of your mental reality. Whatsoever a man thinks becomes his reality. You conquer your storms through the power of reminding the devil of the sovereignty of Jesus Christ.

Remind him that the Word of God says, *"Touch not my anointed and do my prophet no harm."* That's the power of the Word. It is solidified because it is written in God's Word, and nothing can change it. The devil knows this, your storms know this, and your future is waiting for you to pronounce it.

---

*Developing an attitude of steadfastness*
*will help you see beyond your current situation*
*and focus your eyes on the result.*

---

### Release Your Faith

Storms come to also test our faith. James brings us into this knowledge. He clearly stated that *"The testing of your faith produces patience," and we must allow "patience to have its perfect work, that we might become perfect and completely lack nothing"* (James 1:3-4).

You must release your faith to grow in victory. Every faith released must be based on God's Word, and the Word must dominate your faith because faith gets its strength from the Word. No challenge will be conquered without faith. The faith one releases against a situation is stronger and bigger than any obstacles that any situation might cast in your way.

Faith is released by what you hear and what you believe. When you hear the Word of God and believe what you hear, your faith gets bigger, mightier, and stronger. This strength is needed to conquer every mountainous situation in your life.

Your faith is great and mighty. It is the evidence of the Word of God existing in your mind. Your faith is the title deed of power from heaven. It can dominate, uproot, and destroy. Your faith can conquer whatsoever the enemy has brought your way.

Faith is prayer, faith is stronger, and faith is good. Jesus admonished His disciples that if they have faith, just like a mustard seed, they can command a mountain to be removed, and it shall be removed. You can command mountains trying to block you to get out of your way, and it shall be so. That is the power of faith when released.

Faith that is rooted in God's Word dominates your situations as it does your problems. Therefore, rise in faith and stand up with the knowledge that by faith, all things are possible to them that believe.

*When you hear the Word of God and believe what you hear, your faith gets bigger, mightier, and stronger.*

PAYE V. BAGNON

# Chapter 4

# Divine Declarations

## Unleashing the Power of God's Spoken Word
## In the Midst of Life's Storms

One of our greatest abilities is the power of speech, which is why speaking is necessary when releasing your faith. Every challenge you face in life can be stopped by faith that is released through the spoken word. It must be realized that whenever you are releasing your faith, it has to be in line with the Word of God.

The Word of God is powerful when it proceeds from faith within you and is proclaimed by mouth into action against your challenges. The Lord desires us to speak to our dreams, visions, problems, and setbacks because the Word of truth can bring anything into subjection to God's authority.

Do not speak negative words; rather, discipline yourself to start speaking positively. When you release your faith, you must have a positive mindset, outlook, and vision. Your mind must be concentrated on the positive so that positive words can proceed from your mouth.

When you speak the Word of God over your life, you are positioning good over evil, positive over negative, and it results in blessings. No difficult situations should divert your thoughts and cause your tongue to speak negatively when God desires you to speak positively.

No matter what you encounter in your life, whether it is your struggles, unbelief, doubts, disasters, calamities, tragedies, etc., you must go deep within your soul and eradicate the negative thoughts for the goodness of God to be revealed in and through you. God's Word is powerful and strong; it produces everything we need.

*"So shall My word be that goes forth from My mouth; it shall not return to Me void, but it shall accomplish what I please, and it shall prosper in the thing for which I sent it"* (Isaiah 55:11).

Every Word spoken can produce something. Isaiah 53:1 says, *"Whose report will you believe?"* Even if a medical doctor has diagnosed you with a sickness that cannot be healed, whose report will you believe? God has already spoken to us concerning what we are facing. He declares that He will never leave us nor forsake us. That's great news. That's something we can rely on, especially when we face mountains in our life.

He will never leave us or forsake us. When we learn to confess these things from our mouths, we are putting in place the platform necessary for our lives to excel. Our lives will always manifest our thoughts and speech. Therefore, think right and speak right. When this happens, then you will live right. God wants us to dominate our world by speaking great things into our lives.

This is the reason that when we train our tongue to speak good things, then we experience our best life. However, if we speak negative things out of our mouths, our lives become marred or snared by those same confessions. Choose today to turn away from negative words and train your tongue to speak positive words through which the goodness of God can be released in your life.

As you go through your life's storms, do not speak the language of your storm, but rather speak the language of God's Word. Jesus says in the book of Matthew that out of the abundance of the heart, the mouth speaks. Our heart speaks through our mouths, and we are held accountable for what it says.

You must learn to speak orderly things by aligning yourself to success and breakthrough even if you are not seeing it. When you are determined to be positive, you will experience it after a while. Do not allow the constraints of life to dictate how and what to speak. Rather let the Word of God always be your guide.

Don't allow negative situations to overpower you to speak negative words. When you speak negative words, the situation has gained power over you. Speak good things about your life, and positive things will begin to happen.

There was a time when Jesus informed Peter that Satan had asked to get a hold of him to sift him like wheat. Satan always desires to destroy your life, but don't allow Satan to throw you off balance.

You may not understand why you are encountering these setbacks, but while experiencing them, learn to dominate them and the devil by speaking the things that Jesus empowers you to speak. Your tongue is the closest thing to your breakthrough!

Do not be afraid of what you are going through. There is more power in you than you may realize. How you speak determines how God will work things out for you. Refuse to bend your knees to the problems of this world, no matter what they may be. You might face financial problems, marital problems, ministry issues, or other unfavorable circumstances, but remain positive and speak positively.

God responds to you when He hears good and powerful words coming from you. Therefore, stand tall in your mind and spirit, being steadfast, strong, unmovable, and determined. Be relaxed in your faith and act on God's Word.

---

*As you are going through your storms, do not speak the language of your storms, but rather speak the language of God's Word.*

---

Act and agree with the Word. If the devil is after you, you have a responsibility to stand against him. Do you know that no weapon that may be formed against you can prosper, and every tongue that speaks evil or desires harm against you shall be condemned by your own words? You have the power to condemn every attack against you. God has given you this authority.

The truth is, if you do not stand up against the devil for yourself, then who will? If you do not rise up, then who will do it? You are the best prayer warrior of your life. Open your spiritual eyes and see. Develop your spiritual ears and hear. Mature your spiritual mind and perceive the things that God is trying to develop in you.

Agree and act upon the Word of God all the time. When you make this type of decision, it will catapult your life into some tremendous and positive lifestyle habits. You will move higher, run faster, be more steadfast, see further, and become more courageous in your walk with God.

When you agree and act upon the Word of God, you are allowing your spirit to become stronger, and you shall be directed by the positive things of God. The Scriptures say that the steps of the righteous are ordered by the Lord (Psalms 37:23-24). When you agree with God and allow His Word to become active in your life, it will create the space for your solution.

This is a vital step in conquering your storms. The quicker you agree with God, the better the end will be for you. When you make up your mind to agree with God, it means that you trust God in all things. That's one truth the devil hates. It's hard for him to penetrate your faith when you boldly declare that you trust God, even when you don't know what's happening around you.

It makes the devil mad when you trust God during all the storms and hell, he throws at you. When you can do this, you take the power and the sting of the storm away from him. Acting upon God's Word is a warfare declaration that you will not yield to the pressure of Satan's attacks. You are declaring that you will not be confounded or brought into subjection to his negative forces.

The enemy intends to bend you under the pressure and the force of his manipulative witchcraft. However, when you agree with God, you are not allowing the lies or deceptive antics of the enemy to sway you. You are not allowing it to influence your direction in life.

When you do that, you bring the authority in the Word of God to bear on the situation. As such, the enemy knows that you have come into the knowledge of "greater is He that in you—Jesus Christ, than he who is in the world—Satan. He knows he is inferior to Jesus Christ. Keep knocking him down with the Word of God because he belongs under your feet!

The supremacy of God's Word will always overcome your problems because your problems do not affect the Word of God. Once you understand this, you will begin to walk freely concerning the storms you are facing. God's Word has already defeated those storms brought on you by satanic influence.

God's Word is authentic, original, real, and bona fide. It trumps Satan and his agenda every time. You can depend on it, trust it, and make it your confidant. When this truth becomes your living reality, you will not listen to the devil anytime, especially when you have entered a storm. Never listen to your current condition. It might be persistently trying to order your life or convince you of its diabolical plans. No matter the situation, trust God and lean on His Word.

Build a consistent lifestyle of reading and quoting the Word of God. Joshua admonishes us to meditate on the Word of God day and night. He teaches us that the Word of God will make our lives prosperous and successful. We should never let it depart from our mouths! Make a conscious decision to rise and speak the Word of God.

Move forward with the ability the Word provides, and do not allow what you're going through to stop you. You are bigger than your storms, and God is the master of everything, including this moment you find yourself.

---

*God is the master of everything, including*
*this moment in which you find yourself.*

---

### *The Power of Forgiveness*

Storms have a way of making you feel like you amount to nothing. They work on your state of mind to birth your self-defeating thoughts and affirmations. Identify this and rebuke that tendency by cultivating a mountain-moving faith. When you learn how to cultivate a mountain-moving faith, you will have unconsciously also unleashed the power of forgiveness. Learning how to forgive yourself and others is crucial in conquering your storms. Failing to do so will obstruct your deliverance and your ability to conquer your storms. Unforgiveness keeps you trapped in the storms.

*"And whenever you stand praying, if you have anything against anyone, forgive them, that your Father in heaven may also forgive you your trespasses. But if you do not forgive, neither will your Father in heaven forgive your trespasses"* (Mark 11:25-26).

### *Leave the Past in the Past*

You cannot conquer your storms with your past in front of you. Reflecting, for example, on a negative past will keep your mind on that defeated past. Stop shifting the blame on your past mistakes, failures, mishaps, or wrongdoings. Instead, realize that your past mistakes could become good ground for remolding you. The Scripture admonishes us to *"Not remember the former things, neither consider the things of old"* (Isaiah 43:18).

Your past is now behind you, so move forward as a conqueror and leave the past behind you forever. Do not allow the pains of past defeats to continue to hunt you. It's time to leave some things behind. Learn the lessons each storm teaches, but do not live in the storm or carry the storm with you in your mind.

You must learn to leave every weight that holds you down to tap into the blessings that are waiting for you. Every time there is a repeated complaint about something, it creates an open door for Satan to attack. The best you can do to better your future is to leave your failures of the past behind you.

---

*You cannot conquer your storm*
*with your past ahead of you.*

---

### Learn to Praise God

Praising God while facing storms is the best thing you can do. The act of praising God can demolish any satanic prison and get you out of demonic incarceration. The Bible teaches us that while Paul and Silas were incarcerated in Philippi, the jail gates broke open because they began to praise God (Acts 16:25-26). Every time a strong force of storm, trials, and negative experiences happens in your life, use praise as a response.

Praise is a decision to dance, sing, and celebrate Jesus Christ for who He is, what He has done, and what He is about to do. That includes your deliverance. Praise involves appreciating and honoring the Lord for all things.

Praise should not be hypocritical but sincere and honest. The bigger you make your God, the lesser your problems become. Your mind will tell you that your heart is about to fail but let that heart of praise rule the moment.

Are you ready to magnify Him through your storms? Well, the truth is storms are a great place to praise Him. He responds to praise because it sets the atmosphere for Him to enter. When God enters the storms, the power of the storm is destroyed. Psalm 150:6 declares, *"Let everything that has breath praise the Lord."*

So put on your garment of praise, lift your hands, and begin to thank the Lord. The more you praise God, the more you degrade your enemies. The more you exalt Him, the more you edify yourself.

Don't ever quit. Situations will always hit us, and some are harder than others, but there is light at the end of the tunnel. Stand up in your storms, and your testimony will be better than what it has been before.

The devil is clever, but he is not stronger. He might be crafty, but He is not wiser. Jesus is wiser and mightier. Jesus is powerful and stronger. The higher your problem, the closer you should draw closer to God and establish His presence around you.

Know God during your storms. Know that He will come through for you amid your storms, and the storms will not go through you.

---

***The more you praise God,
the more you degrade your enemies.***

---

PAYE V. BAGNON

# Chapter 5

# Unraveling Misconceptions

## Understanding the Purpose and Promise of Life's Storms

There are many reasons why people may have misunderstandings about life's storms. Below are some of the reasons.

### 1. Unrealistic Expectations About Life

Many people expect life to be smooth and easy without challenges or difficulties, but that is not the case. Jesus clearly pointed to the fact that; in this world, we shall face trials and tribulations (John 16:33). People with unrealistic expectations of life, when faced with a storm, may feel overwhelmed and unable to handle it.

### 2. Necessary Skills or Resources to Deal With Life's Storms

Many people are unprepared when it comes to handling difficult situations. For example, they may lack a family and friends support network, or they may not have the financial means to weather a crisis. In such cases, they may feel helpless and hopeless in the face of a storm.

### 3. Limited Perspective of Life

Many people are in the habit of focusing only on their own experiences and not considering the challenges and struggles that others face. They may also have a narrow understanding of what it means to be successful or happy, believing that happiness and success are only possible in the absence of difficulties.

### 4. Misconceptions About the Nature of Storms

Many people may believe that storms are always negative or destructive when in fact, they can be opportunities for growth and transformation that could strengthen our relationship with God.

Overall, misunderstandings about life's storms can stem from various factors, including unrealistic expectations, a lack of resources or skills, limited perspective, and misconceptions about the nature of storms. By gaining a more accurate understanding of life's storms, people can better prepare themselves to face and overcome challenges.

---

*By gaining a more accurate understanding of life's storms, we can better prepare ourselves to face and overcome challenges.*

---

### Job's Experience

After Job was battered by a series of devastating tragedies, his sympathizing friends traveled a great distance to be with him. This is a common scenario each time disaster strikes.

His friends sat silently with him for seven days and nights, staying by his side during his grief. Of course, when something like this happens, everyone has their own perceptions about the situation. Many people will misjudge the situation or even you, the victim, based on the occurrence or speculations. Still, your silence and prayers are the best way to go.

Job finally broke the silence, saying, *"The thing which I greatly feared is come upon me"* (Job3:25). With this statement, Job lamented that the worst tragedy he could imagine had happened to him. At this point, Job has discovered the reality of storms.

It is important to note that most unseen realities resurface when people you thought could support you begin to misjudge you because of the intensity of the moment's devastating, destitute, and unbearable pains.

Many of us have wondered what we would do if a tragedy occurred. For some, this would be the death of a spouse or perhaps the loss of a child, a loss in ministry, a loss of an opportunity, or a loss of a relationship. For others, it could be a cancer diagnosis or the loss of mental capacity. Yet, for others, it could be a damaging fire or other catastrophe.

Psalm 46 is a powerful reminder of God's strength and presence in the midst of life's storms. The psalm begins with the declaration, *"God is our refuge and strength, an ever-present help in trouble"* (Psalms 46:1 NIV).

This verse sets the tone for the entire psalm, emphasizing that God is always our source of strength and security, especially during times of difficulty. The psalm goes on to describe various kinds of turmoil and chaos, including natural disasters and political upheavals.

Despite these challenges, the psalmist remains confident in God's power and protection. He finally declares, *"Be still, and know that*

*I am God; I will be exalted among the nations, I will be exalted in the earth"* (Psalms 46:10 NIV).

This verse encourages us to trust in God's sovereignty and to recognize that He is ultimately in control, even when everything around us is in turmoil.

In the midst of life's storms, Psalm 46 can be a source of comfort and hope. It reminds us that we are not alone and that God is always with us, providing strength and protection. It encourages us to trust in God's power and be still, knowing He is in control. For instance, it declares that:

*"God is our refuge and strength, an ever-present help in trouble. Therefore we will not fear, though the Earth give way and the mountains fall into the heart of the sea, Though its waters roar and foam and the mountains quake with their surging. There is a river whose streams make glad the city of God, the holy place where the Most High dwells. God is within her, she will not fall; God will help her at the break of day. Nations are in uproar, kingdoms fall; he lifts his voice, the Earth melts. The LORD Almighty is with us; the God of Jacob is our fortress. Come and see what the LORD has done, the desolations he has brought on the Earth. He makes wars cease to the ends of the Earth. He breaks the bow and shatters the spear; he burns the shields with fire. He says, "Be still, and know that I am God; I will be exalted among the nations, I will be exalted in the Earth. The LORD Almighty is with us; the God of Jacob is our fortress."*

Ultimately, Psalm 46 reminds us that wisdom demands we trust in God and find our security and strength in Him. *Be still* because life is often very cruel; hopes that have risen to great heights crash to the ground in disappointment. Everywhere, every day, thousands of people are facing:

1. Disease
2. Loss of job
3. Deformity
4. Shortage of money
5. Accident
6. Bankruptcy
7. Suffering
8. Broken relationship
9. Death

### *Deploying Faith and Tack in Warding off Storms*

The cry of the heart at such moments is, "Where is God when we really need Him?" Storms of life come with accusations and misconceptions about your personality and even about your faith but learn to use silence and prayers as your tools to overcome these unfortunate moments.

Your acquaintances, friends, children in the Lord, church members, and even those you trust and have helped will run away from you. When this happens, know that you are not alone in this, for the comforter, the Holy Spirit, is always with you.

Also, be assured that the storm is just a passing moment of life, such that at a certain point, everything will be fine. In the face of declining investments, ministry, family crises, and more, remember that you are stronger than what you face.

Most people who have never experienced the nature of your storms will always misjudge you. In such moments, be prepared for anything but don't allow bitterness to keep you locked away from forgiving those who will injure you in the process.

---

*We are not alone. God is always with us,*
*providing strength and protection.*

---

# Chapter 6

# Through The Tempest

### Embracing the Experience of Life's Storms

Regrettably, suffering is an aspect of life shared by everyone. At any given moment, you must realize that millions of people all over the world are going through problems—facing obstacles, enduring pains of all kinds, and bearing heavy burdens.

*Suffering socially:* Many people are being treated like outcasts-rejected, ridiculed, mocked, ignored, and neglected.

*Suffering Physically:* Many have been injured in a fight, a war, an assault, or a serious accident. Others have been afflicted with a serious disease or disability.

*Suffering Spiritually:* Many have rejected God outright and are plagued by guilt, or at the very least, they are unsure if there is a future life in heaven or hell. Others feel abandoned or forsaken by God because their prayers seem to go unanswered. They feel distant and cut off from God by living sinful lifestyles and failing to obey God's holy commandments.

*Suffering Emotionally:* For many reasons, people are saturated by sorrow, despair, depression, guilt, loss of a spouse or loved one.

Sometimes the reasons for emotional suffering are legitimate, and at other times they are irrational. Whatever the cause, an emotional disturbance is very real to the sufferers.

### *Spiritual Experience*

The spiritual experience of a storm of life can vary greatly depending on one's personal beliefs, experiences, and perspectives. Some people may view the storms of life as a test of faith or an opportunity for personal growth and transformation. They may see it to deepen one's connection with God and gain a greater sense of purpose and meaning in life.

However, others may view a storm of life as a challenge to their beliefs or as a sign of spiritual abandonment by God. They may feel anger, frustration, or despair in the face of adversity and struggle to find meaning or purpose in their suffering.

Regardless of one's perspective, storms of life can be powerful catalysts for spiritual growth and development, forcing us to confront our deepest fears and insecurities so we can let go of what no longer serves us and embrace new ways of living and thinking.

Ultimately, the spiritual experience of a storm of life is a deeply personal and individual journey that requires courage, resilience and an unwavering commitment to personal growth and transformation.

In the book of Job, chapter 30, Job describes his spiritual experience as one of deep anguish and despair. He compares his current state to his previous life of prosperity and honor, which he now sees as a distant memory. Job laments the loss of his wealth, health, and status, and he feels abandoned by God.

> *Storms of life can be powerful catalysts for spiritual growth and development, forcing us to confront our deepest fears and insecurities so we can let go of what no longer serves us, and embrace new ways of living and thinking.*

Job describes his suffering in vivid detail, using metaphors such as *"my bones burn with fever"* (Job 30:30) and *"my days have passed away, my plans are broken off, even the desires of my heart"* (Job 30:27).

Job feels isolated and alone, rejected by his friends and family, and he cries out to God for help but receives no answer. Despite his deep despair, Job retains his faith in God and his belief in divine justice.

He believes that his suffering is not deserved, and that God will eventually vindicate him. He expresses this trust in God when he says, *"Though he slay me, yet will I trust him" (Job 13:15).*

Overall, Job's spiritual experience in Job 30 is one of intense suffering and despair but also of unwavering faith in God's justice and mercy. Storms of life can profoundly impact us spiritually as they challenge our beliefs, values, and sense of purpose. Here are some ways that storms of life can impact us spiritually:

*1. Deepening Our Faith*

The storms of life can be opportunities to deepen our connection with God. They can force us to confront our beliefs and develop a more profound and meaningful relationship with God.

## 2. Testing our Faith

The storms of life can also test our beliefs and values, forcing us to re-evaluate our faith and why we should have faith. They can challenge us to develop our faith and embrace new ways of thinking and being.

## 3. Fostering Spiritual Growth

The storms of life can be catalysts for spiritual growth and transformation. They can compel us to confront our fears and insecurities and develop new levels of resilience, courage, and compassion.

## 4. Developing Empathy And Compassion

The storms of life can also help us develop greater empathy and compassion for others who are suffering. They can deepen our understanding of the human condition and our interconnectedness with others.

## 5. Providing A Sense Of Purpose

Life's storms can also give us a sense of purpose and meaning. They can help us to see our lives in a larger context and to understand how our experiences can be used to serve others and to make a positive impact in the world. The storms of life can be challenging and difficult experiences. Still, they can also be powerful opportunities for spiritual growth, transformation, and healing.

---

*Storms of life can be challenging and difficult experiences, but they can also be powerful opportunities for spiritual growth, transformation, and healing.*

---

### *Commitment In the Storm*

Despite his difficulties, Job remained faithful to God, and in the end, God restored his fortunes and blessed him with even more than he had before. The book of Job highlights the importance of prayer and the power of God to bring restoration and blessings to those who trust in Him.

The storm in Job's life was a time of great trial and suffering. Still, through his faithfulness and trust in God, he could ultimately overcome and receive blessings beyond what he could have imagined. This story is a powerful reminder of the importance of faith and perseverance in the face of difficult circumstances and the hope we can have in God's ability to bring restoration and blessing into our lives.

Life's storms can be referred to as a variety of challenging or difficult experiences that we encounter, such as illness, loss, financial struggles, relationship challenges, or other forms of adversities. These storms can be emotionally and physically draining, often leaving us feeling overwhelmed, exhausted, and uncertain about the future.

Physically, the experience of life's storms can manifest in various ways. For example, chronic stress or anxiety related to these experiences can lead to physical symptoms such as headaches, muscle tension, and digestive issues.

Depression, grief, and other emotional struggles can also impact our physical health, leading to changes in appetite, sleep disorders, and fatigue. Moreover, life's storms can also impact our physical environment by disrupting our daily routines and activities.

For example, a serious illness may require hospitalization and medical treatment, leading to a significant change in our daily activities and routines and financial disruption. Similarly, financial struggles may require us to adjust our spending habits or even move to a new home or location.

Overall, the physical experience of life's storms can be incredibly challenging. However, it is still important to remember that we can take steps to care for ourselves and seek support from others during these difficult times.

The pain of life's storms can be intense and overwhelming. These storms can bring about a wide range of emotions, including sadness, anger, fear, and anxiety. For example, the loss of a loved one can bring about intense grief and sadness, while financial struggles can lead to feelings of anxiety and uncertainty about the future.

The pain of life's storms can also manifest physically, as chronic stress and emotional distress can impact our physical health. This may include headaches, muscle tension, digestive issues, chest pain, and other physical symptoms.

Moreover, life's storms can challenge our sense of identity and purpose, leading to feelings of confusion, self-doubt, and a loss of direction. This can be particularly difficult when faced with sudden or unexpected changes, such as job loss, divorce, or serious illness.

It is important to acknowledge and validate the pain of these experiences, as suppressing or denying our emotions can lead to further distress and negatively impact our health and well-being. Seeking support from loved ones or professional mental health service providers can be helpful when coping with the pain of life's storms. Still, the most useful engagement will be with the Word of God.

God's Word can build up daily as you navigate through your storms. You can also find ways to engage in self-care, listening to music and activities that bring us joy and fulfillment.

### Physical Experience of the Storms

Job chapter 30 is a portion of Scripture where Job laments his current state of suffering and compares it to the life he had previously enjoyed. He describes his current situation as a "life's storm," using powerful imagery to convey the intensity and devastation of his suffering. Overall, Job Chapter 30 provides a vivid and powerful description of the experience of suffering and the impact it can have on all aspects of a person's life.

According to Job chapter 30, the social experience of life's storms can be very isolating and lonely. Job describes how his friends and acquaintances have abandoned him in his time of need and how he is now mocked and ridiculed by those who were once his peers.

In Job 30:1-14, Job talks about how he has become an outcast in his community, saying,

*"But now they mock me, men who are younger than I, whose fathers I would have disdained to set with the dogs of my flock."*

He goes on to say that he has been pushed to the margins of society, forced to live in the wilderness and scavenge for food. Job also talks about how his suffering has impacted on his relationships with his family. In Job 30:15-22, he describes how his brothers and sisters have turned against him and how his closest friends have abandoned him.

*"My brothers are treacherous as a torrent-bed, as torrential streams that pass away, which are dark with ice, and where the snow hides itself. When they melt, they disappear; when it is hot,*

*they vanish from their place. The caravans turn aside from their course; they go up into the waste and perish."*

Overall, Job's social experience of life's storms is one of rejection, isolation, and abandonment. His suffering caused him to lose his place in society and damaged his relationships with those around him.

According to Job chapter 30, the physical experience of life's storms can be very intense and painful. Job describes how his body is racked with pain and how he suffered from various physical afflictions.

In Job 30:16-19, he describes his physical pain and the emotional toll it is taking on him, saying, *"And now my soul is poured out within me; days of affliction have taken hold of me. The night racks my bones, and the pain that gnaws at me takes no rest. With violence, it seizes my garment; it binds me about like the collar of my tunic. God has cast me into the mire, and I have become like dust and ashes."*

Job goes on to describe the specific physical afflictions he is experiencing. In Job 30:27-31, he talks about how his skin has turned black and is peeling off, his bones are burning with fever, and he is suffering from constant nausea and vomiting.

*"My skin turns black and falls from me, and my bones burn with heat. My lyre is turned to mourning and my pipe to the voice of those who weep. I am a brother of jackals and a companion of ostriches. My skin turns black and falls from me, and my bones burn with heat. Therefore, my harp is turned to mourning and my pipe to the voice of those who weep."*

Job experienced a variety of physical afflictions that caused him great distress, both physically and emotionally. Despite his storms and against all odds, Job held tightly to God and endured.

Eventually, his endurance paid off as he saw God answer his prayers. God turned Job's sadness into joy and restored everything Job lost and more. As we consider all that Job endured, it provides perspective for our own storms. If God can do it for Job, He can do it for us, also.

---

*As we consider all that Job endured; it*
*provides perspective for our own storms.*
*If God can do it for Job, He can do it for us also.*

---

PAYE V. BAGNON

# Chapter 7

# Songs In The Storm

## Finding Strength through Worship and Praise
## In Life's Toughest Moments

Are you able to worship God in hard times? This is one of the most difficult tasks of the faith life. It is easy to worship God when the sun shines bright. It is easy to worship God when things are going well, but what about during hard times? Job gives us an excellent example of someone who could worship God during an unusually hard time.

The Word of God says in Job 1:21 that after experiencing tremendous loss, *"Job got up and tore his robe and shaved his head. Then he fell to the ground and worshipped."* In Job 1:22, we read the words that Job expressed as he worshipped God; *"Naked I came from my mother's womb, and naked I will depart. The LORD gave and the LORD has taken away; may the name of the LORD be praised."*

Job lost his children, his land, and most of his possessions, yet he worshipped God.

### *Worship is Being Honest with God*

We learn from Job's response that worship is not only carried out when you have the feeling. You may have wondered why you are worshipping in the midst of other believers, and yet you didn't feel anything."

If worship is only based on a feeling, what happens when we face devastating circumstances in which we do not feel like it? Does that mean our faith goes dormant during such times? Worship actually means anything we do that gives glory to God. If that is what worship is, then it cannot be based on feelings.

Also, worship cannot be based on circumstances. Job found himself in a sequence of unfavorable circumstances and suffered tremendous loss, yet he worshipped God. Throughout the Bible, we see expressions of praise that grew out of difficult circumstances.

The writers of Psalms did so during pain, heartache, and suffering. Paul wrote the book of Philippians from captivity, yet the theme of the book of Philippians is "joy." John wrote Revelation while in exile, yet the theme of Revelation is "victory."

---

*If worship is only based on feeling, then what happens when we face devastating circumstances in which we do not feel like it?*

---

### *Worship is Trusting God*

Job lost most of his worldly possessions, yet he continued to trust God. In trusting God during the hard times, we are simply declaring His sovereignty. In doing so, we are trusting God's plans for our lives.

The Bible says, *"For My thoughts are not your thoughts, Nor are your ways My ways," says the Lord. "For as the heavens are higher than the earth, So are My ways higher than your ways, And My thoughts than your thoughts"* (Isaiah 55:8-9).

Worship is an act of faith and is not always based on convenience. But regardless, faith does not always get easy answers, but it leads you to the best answer for your situation. Faith is an act of obedience in the same manner as any other act of obedience toward God.

When Jesus went to the cross, He did it as an act of obedience, not because it was convenient. If faith is an act of obedience, it must be performed as an act of our will. Sometimes it will not make sense, and it is often not easy. Someone once said, "I do what is right because it is right until it feels right."

Worship in the storms of life refers to praising and giving thanks to God during difficult or challenging circumstances. It is a way of expressing faith and trust in God's ability to see us through any situation.

When we encounter storms in life, whether they are physical, emotional, or spiritual, it can be easy to become overwhelmed or discouraged. However, turning to worship can help us focus on God's power and presence and find strength and hope amid our struggles.

Worship can take many forms, such as singing hymns or songs, praying, reading Scriptures, or simply meditating on God's goodness and faithfulness. Whatever form it takes, worship can serve as a powerful reminder that we are not alone in our struggles and that God is always with us, guiding and sustaining us through even the toughest times.

*Turning to worship can help us focus on God's power and Presence, and find strength and hope in the midst of our struggles.*

In the Bible, we see numerous examples of people who worshipped God in the midst of difficult circumstances. Such examples include Job, who praised God even after losing everything he had, and Paul and Silas, who sang hymns even while in prison. These examples remind us that worship can be a source of strength and comfort even in our darkest moments.

Job 1:20-21 is a passage in the Bible that speaks to us about worshiping God during difficult circumstances. It reads, *"Then Job arose, tore his robe, and shaved his head, and he fell to the ground and worshipped. And he said, 'Naked I came from my mother's womb, and naked shall I return there. The Lord gave, and the Lord has taken away; blessed be the name of the Lord."*

We see Job reacting to the news that he lost all his children and possessions. Despite the immense pain and grief that he must be feeling, Job chose to worship God instead of turning away from him. Job's actions in this passage demonstrate a deep trust in God's sovereignty and goodness, even in the face of overwhelming losses.

By worshiping God, Job acknowledges that everything he has in his life comes from God and that God has the power to take it away. He also recognizes that God is still worthy of praise and adoration, regardless of his circumstances.

This passage serves as a powerful reminder that, even amid the most difficult storms of life, we can choose to worship God and find comfort and strength in His presence. We can find hope and peace amid our struggles by fixing our eyes on God and praising him.

### *Worship is Standing Firm in the Face of Adversity*

Acts 16:25-40 is another passage in the Bible that speaks about the idea of worshiping God during great adversity. This passage shows Paul and Silas imprisoned in Philippi for preaching the gospel. Despite being beaten and thrown into prison, they worship God through singing and prayer.

In Acts 16:25-40, we read, *"Paul and Silas were praying and singing hymns to God about midnight, and the other prisoners were listening to them. Suddenly there was such a violent earthquake that the prison's foundations were shaken. All the prison doors flew open at once, and everyone's chains came loose. The jailer woke up, and when he saw the prison doors open, he drew his sword and was about to kill himself because he thought the prisoners had escaped. But Paul shouted, "Don't harm yourself! We are all here!" The jailer called for lights, rushed in, and fell trembling before Paul and Silas. He brought them out and asked, "Sirs, what must I do to be saved?" They replied, "Believe in the Lord Jesus, and you will be saved—you and your household." Then they spoke the word of the Lord to him and to all the others in his house. At that hour of the night, the jailer took them and washed their wounds, then immediately, he and all his household were baptized. The jailer brought them into his house and set a meal before them; he was filled with joy because he had come to believe in God—he and his whole household. When it was daylight, the magistrates sent their officers to the jailer with the order: "Release those men." The jailer told Paul, "The magistrates have ordered that you and Silas be released. Now you can leave. Go in peace." But Paul told the officers: "They beat us publicly without a trial, even though we are Roman citizens, and threw us into prison. And now, do they want to get rid of us quietly? No! Let them come themselves and escort us out." The officers reported this to the magistrates, and when they heard that Paul and Silas were Roman citizens, they were alarmed. They came to appease them and escorted them from the prison, requesting them to leave the city. After Paul and Silas exited the prison, they went to Lydia's house, where they met with the brothers and sisters and encouraged them. Then they left."*

We see Paul and Silas worshiping God amid difficult circumstances, even as they are imprisoned. Their worship ultimately leads to their release from prison, as well as the conversion of the jailer and his household to Christianity. This passage is a powerful reminder that worshiping God amid trials can bring about unexpected blessings and miracles.

---

***Worshiping God in the midst of trials can bring about unexpected blessings and miracles.***

---

Psalm 42 is a beautiful expression of worship and praise during life's storms. The psalmist begins by expressing his deep longing for God, comparing it to his thirst for water in a dry and thirsty land. The psalmist is clearly going through a difficult time, feeling oppressed and overwhelmed by his circumstances.

That Scripture says, *"As the deer pants for streams of water, so my soul pants for you, my God. My soul thirsts for God, for the living God. When can I go and meet with God? My tears have been my food day and night, while people say to me all day long, "Where is your God?" These things I remember as I pour out my soul: how I used to go to the house of God under the protection of the Mighty One with shouts of joy and praise among the festive throng. Why, my soul, are you downcast? Why so disturbed within me? Put your hope in God, for yet I will praise him, my Savior, and my God. My soul is downcast within me; therefore, I will remember you from the land of the Jordan, the heights of Hermon—from Mount Mizar. Deep calls to deep in the roar of your waterfalls; all your waves and breakers have swept over me. By day the LORD directs his love, at night his song is with me—a prayer to the God of my life. I say to God, my Rock, "Why have you forgotten me? Why must I go about mourning, oppressed by the enemy?" My bones suffer mortal agony as my foes taunt me, saying to me all day long, "Where is your God?" Why, my soul, are you downcast? Why so disturbed within me? Put your hope in God, for I will yet praise him, my Savior and my God"* (Psalms 42:1-11).

Despite his struggles, however, the psalmist does not lose faith in God. He remembers the times when he felt close to God when he worshipped and praised Him with joy and gladness. He longs to experience that same closeness again, so he pours his heart to God in prayer and song.

Throughout the psalm, the psalmist acknowledges his pain and sorrow. Still, he also affirms his trust in God's goodness and faithfulness. He knows that God is his rock and salvation and that even in the midst of the storm, he can find refuge in God's love and grace.

The psalmist's example reminds us that we can still worship and praise God even when life is hard. We can pour out our hearts to Him, expressing our deepest fears and struggles and trusting that He hears our prayers and cares for us deeply. We can remember the times when God has been faithful to us in the past and hold on to the hope that He will continue to be faithful.

Ultimately, Psalm 42 teaches us that worship and praise are not just expressions of joy and happiness but also of faith and trust in God, even during life's storms. We should note that the psalmist refused to give in to his depression, choosing instead to battle it by remembering God. Let's consider three life-changing lessons from Psalm 42 that can help us when we are bound by despair.

## 1. Worship is Focusing on the Truth

First, the psalmist focused on the truth of God's Word rather than the lies of the tormentor of his soul. Overwhelmed by his troubles, the psalmist felt that God had forgotten him. But this was not true! The truth was he was surrounded by God's unfailing love even amid his problems.

One of the most effective ways Satan attacks us is through our minds by lying to us through our flawed and often foolish thinking. The fact is that many of the doubts that plague us are simply not true. They are the imaginations of our minds, which are thoughts contrary to what we know about God. Scripture teaches that we must take these thoughts captive and subject them to the obedience of Christ.

*"We demolish arguments and every pretension that sets itself up against the knowledge of God, and we take captive every thought to make it obedient to Christ"* (2 Corinthians 10:5).

And then we are commanded to focus our minds on the things that are true, pure, and of good report. *"Finally, brothers and sisters, whatever is true, whatever is noble, whatever is right, whatever is pure, whatever is lovely, whatever is admirable—if anything is excellent or praiseworthy—think about such things"* (Philippians 4:8).

## 2. Focus on God's Unfailing Love Even in the Midst of Trouble

The psalmist recognized God's goodness and clung to God's mercy in his sea of discouragement. No matter how bad things may get in our lives, God loves us and is good to us. We are reminded of the power of God's love in Romans 8:38-39, which reads:

*"For I am convinced that neither death nor life, neither angels nor demons, neither the present nor the future, nor any powers, neither height nor depth nor anything else in all creation, will be able to separate us from the love of God that is in Christ Jesus our Lord."*

### 3. Chose to Praise God From Your Depth of Depression

Praising God lifted the psalmist out of the depths of despair, putting a smile on his face and giving him a song in his heart. Praise is truly powerful. As our praise blesses the LORD, it also changes us.

---

***Praise is powerful. As our praise blesses the Lord, and it also changes us.***

---

Psalm 43 is a continuation of the themes found in Psalm 42, with the psalmist expressing his deep longing for God's presence and deliverance during difficult circumstances. The psalmist begins by pleading with God to vindicate him against his enemies, who are oppressing him and causing him great distress.

*"Vindicate me, my God, and plead my cause against an unfaithful nation. Rescue me from those who are deceitful and wicked. You are God, my stronghold. Why have you rejected me? Why must I go about mourning, oppressed by the enemy? Send me your light and your faithful care, let them lead me; let them bring me to your holy mountain, to the place where you dwell. Then I will go to the altar of God, to God, my joy and my delight. I will praise you with the lyre, O God, my God. Why, my soul, are you downcast? Why so disturbed within me? Put your hope in God, for I will yet praise him, my Savior and my God"* (Psalms 43:1-5).

Despite his struggles, the psalmist does not lose faith in God's goodness and faithfulness. He declares his trust in God's salvation and commitment to worship and praise Him even amid the storms. The psalmist recognizes that God is his stronghold and his refuge and that he can find hope and strength in God's presence.

The psalmist acknowledges his pain and sorrow but also affirms his confidence in God's love and mercy. He knows that God is his light and his truth and that even amid darkness and confusion, he can trust in God's guidance and direction.

The psalmist's example reminds us that worship and praise are not just expressions of joy and happiness, but also of faith and trust in God, even amid life's storms. We can cry out to God in prayer, expressing our deepest fears and struggles. We can trust that He hears our cries and cares for us deeply.

We can remember the times when God has been faithful to us in the past and hold onto the hope that He will continue to be faithful. Psalm 43 teaches us that worship and praise are powerful tools for navigating the storms of life.

When we choose to worship and praise God during our struggles, we invite His presence and power into our lives, and we are reminded of His faithfulness and love. At various times in our lives, we may find ourselves trapped in situations where we have no control.

Like the psalmist, we may be victims of slander or false judgment by people who want to hurt us. Or, we may be facing a grave illness, marital or family problems, financial crises, or the death of a loved one.

At some point in time, we will all know the feeling of being powerless to change an extremely grievous situation. When we reach the end of ourselves and our abilities, we must remember that God can do what we cannot. His strength is revealed through our weaknesses and inabilities.

Thankfully, He invites us to come boldly to His holy throne to seek grace and mercy to help us in our time of need. *"Let us then approach God's throne of grace with confidence so that we may receive mercy and find grace to help us in our time of need"* (Hebrews 4:16).

When under the pressure of crushing circumstances, we are prone to question God's love and care for us. It is easy to feel that He has rejected or forsaken us. In such times, we must rest in His promise that "He will never leave or forsake us." He promises to stand by us in the fiery trials of life.

We may not always understand why God permits us to face grievous situations, but we can be sure that He does not allow us to go through them alone. Consider Shadrach, Meshach, and Abednego's experience in the fiery furnace. In Daniel 3:1-30 we learn that, for the fact that God was with these faithful servants of His in their time of dire need, they were delivered from the fire. He is surely with us and will also deliver us.

Daniel 3:1-30 tells the story of Shadrach, Meshach, and Abednego, three young Jewish men who refused to worship a golden image set up by King Nebuchadnezzar of Babylon. The king threatened to throw them into the furnace if they did not comply, but the three men refused to bow down to anyone or anything other than the one true God.

In the face of this great trial, Shadrach, Meshach, and Abednego demonstrated incredible faith and trust in God. They knew that God was able to deliver them from the fire, but even if He did not, they were still committed to worshiping and serving Him alone.

The three young men were thrown into a furnace that was seven times hotter than ordinary, and they sang and praised God, declaring His power and sovereignty over all things. Even as the flames raged around them, they did not waver in their faith but continued worshiping and praising God.

God honored their faith and delivered them from the fire, causing King Nebuchadnezzar to marvel at the power of the God of Israel.

The story of Shadrach, Meshach, and Abednego reminds us that worship and praise are powerful weapons while experiencing the storms of life. When we choose to worship and praise God amid our struggles, we invite His presence and power into our lives, and we are reminded of His faithfulness and love.

Like Shadrach, Meshach, and Abednego, we can trust in God's power and goodness, even amid the fiery trials we face. When we choose to worship and praise Him, we declare our faith in His ability to deliver and sustain us, no matter what may come our way.

---

*We can trust that God hears our*
*cries and cares for us deeply.*

---

### Worship is Acknowledging God in the Face of Danger

There is a wonderful story found in 2 Chronicles 20 about King Jehoshaphat of Judah and how he responded when he was faced with a great threat from a coalition of enemy armies. In the face of this imminent danger, Jehoshaphat did not panic or turn to military might for help. Instead, he turned to God in prayer and fasting, seeking His guidance and protection throughout Judah, and calling on the people to seek the Lord.

He stood before the people and prayed aloud, acknowledging God's power and sovereignty over all creation and the trustworthiness of His promises. Jehoshaphat reminded God of His covenant with His people and the promises He had made to protect them. Jehoshaphat also expressed his own trust in God's ability to deliver them from their enemies.

In response to Jehoshaphat's prayer, the Holy Spirit came upon a Levite named Jahaziel. He prophesied that the battle belonged to God and that they need not fight. God instructed them to position themselves and watch the salvation of the Lord.

Jehoshaphat and the people of Judah responded with worship and praise, and as they began to sing and give thanks, the Lord caused their enemies to turn on each other and destroy themselves.

This account in God's Word teaches us the power of seeking God in prayer and worship, even during life's storms and challenges. When we face difficulties, we can turn to God in faith and trust that He will guide and protect us.

We can also take comfort in the fact that God is faithful to keep His promises and deliver us from our enemies. Therefore, we should always be ready to offer worship and praise to God, regardless of our circumstances.

### *Worship Makes a Way Through Your Storm*

Psalm 34 provides a beautiful expression of worship and praise to God in the midst of life's storms. The author, David, wrote this psalm after he had been through a very difficult time in his life, and he wanted to share his experience of God's faithfulness with others.

*"I will extol the LORD at all times; his praise will always be on my lips. I will glory in the LORD; let the afflicted hear and rejoice. Glorify the LORD with me; let us exalt his name together. I sought the LORD, and he answered me; he delivered me from all my fears. Those who look to him are radiant; their faces are never covered with shame. This poor man called, and the LORD heard him; he saved him out of all his troubles. The angel of the LORD encamps around those who fear him, and he delivers them. Taste and see that the LORD is good; blessed is the one who takes refuge in him. Fear the LORD, you his holy people, for those who fear him lack nothing. The lions may grow weak and hungry, but those who seek the LORD lack no good thing. Come, my children, listen to me; I will teach you the fear of the LORD. Whoever of you loves life and desires to see many good days, keep your tongue from evil and your lips from telling lies. Turn from evil and do good; seek peace and pursue it. The eyes of the LORD are on the righteous, and his ears are attentive to their cry; but the face of the LORD is against those who do evil, to blot out their name from the Earth. The righteous cry out, and the LORD hears them; he delivers them from all their troubles. The LORD is close to the broken-hearted and saves those who are crushed in spirit. The righteous person may have many troubles, but the LORD delivers him from them all; he protects all his bones, and not one of them will be broken. Evil will slay the wicked; the foes of the righteous will be condemned. The LORD will rescue his servants; no one who takes refuge in him will be condemned"* (Psalm 34:1-22).

In verses 1-4, David begins by expressing his gratitude and praise to God for His goodness and faithfulness. He encourages others to join him in worshiping God and testifying to His greatness. David acknowledges that God has delivered him from his fears and troubles and that his soul is filled with joy and peace because of God's presence in his life. God will deliver you from your fears as you express gratitude in worship.

In verses 5-7, David reflects on his personal experience of God's deliverance. He acknowledges that he has been in a desperate situation, but God heard his cry for help and rescued him. David encourages others to trust in God, saying that those who look to Him are radiant with joy and will never be disappointed.

Just like it was with David, when you worship God, you will discover your mood will lift, and God will renew your hope.

In verses 8-10, David encourages others to trust in God and seek Him for their needs. He assures them that God is always near to those who call on Him and that He will rescue them from their troubles.

As you engage in the act of worship, it is important to note that nothing is missing. A divine provision is made for recovery, restoration, and the manifestation of everything you once lost.

In the remaining verses of the psalm, David gives practical advice for living a life that is pleasing to God. He encourages us to fear the Lord, turn from evil, seek peace, and pursue it. He reminds us that the eyes of the Lord are on the righteous and that He hears their prayers.

---

*Just like it was with David, when you worship God, you will discover your mood will lift, and God will renew your hope.*

---

Overall, Psalm 34 is a powerful expression of worship and praise to God during life's storms. It reminds us that even when we face difficulties, we can trust in God's goodness and faithfulness and that worshiping and praising Him brings us joy, peace, and deliverance.

Worship and praise play a crucial role in helping us navigate the storms of life. When we face challenges, we can turn to God in prayer and worship, acknowledging His power and sovereignty over all creation. We can express our trust in His ability to deliver us from our enemies and guide us through difficult times.

In summary, worship, and praise help us to focus on God's goodness and faithfulness, even when we face challenges and difficulties. God is always near to those who call on Him, so He hears our prayers and can deliver us from our enemies and guide us through difficult times.

As we worship and praise, we discover the storms begin to calm, and the light of God begins to shine through into our hearts, and it gives us an inner peace that creates hope for the future.

---

*God knows the battles you are facing in your life's storms and will make a way for you to overcome them as you worship Him.*

---

## Chapter 8

# A New Dawn

### Restoration and Renewal amid Life's Toughest Storms

Restoration is a word that suggests recovering or renewing someone or something, and in this case, restoring oneself even amid difficult or challenging circumstances. Life can be unpredictable and even chaotic, and it's important to find ways to weather the storms that come our way.

One way to find restoration in the storm of life is to practice self-care. This can involve taking time for activities that bring us joy and relaxation, such as exercise, meditation, and reading. Others are listening to music, praying, or spending time with loved ones.

It may also mean seeking support from friends, family, your pastor, or a mental health professional when struggling with difficult emotions or experiences. However, you must be aware that the Holy Spirit is always there to help you.

Another way to find restoration is to focus on the things we can control rather than things beyond our control. For example, we may not be able to control the challenges that come our way, but we can control how we respond to them. We can find a sense of empowerment even amid difficult circumstances by focusing on our thoughts, feelings, and actions.

Finding restoration in the storms of life may involve re-evaluating our priorities and making changes to create a more balanced and fulfilled life. This means letting go of things that no longer serve us, such as unhealthy relationships or stressful jobs, and focusing on the things that bring us joy and fulfillment.

> *Finding restoration in the storms of life may involve re-evaluating your priorities and making changes to create a more balanced and fulfilled life.*

Learn to reposition yourself to create a genuine relationship with God. In Isaiah 43:18-19 we read, *"Forget the former things; do not dwell on the past. See, I am doing a new thing! Now it springs up; do you not perceive it? I am making a way in the wilderness and streams in the wasteland."*

This passage speaks to the idea of restoration during difficult circumstances. It encourages us to let go of the past and focus on the present and future, where God is doing something new. The "way in the wilderness" and "streams in the wasteland" suggest that even in the most challenging situations, God can provide a way forward and bring new life and growth.

This passage can be a source of hope and encouragement for those going through difficult times, reminding them that God is always at work, even when things seem hopeless or bleak. It also encourages us to trust God's provision and guidance, even when we can't see the way forward.

*"You shall eat in plenty and be satisfied, and praise the name of the Lord your God, who has dealt wondrously with you. And my people shall never again be put to shame. You shall know that I am in the midst of Israel, and that I am the Lord your God and there is no other. And it shall come to pass afterward, that I will pour out my Spirit on all flesh; your sons and your daughters shall prophesy, your old men shall dream dreams, and your young men shall see visions"* (Joel 2:26-28).

This passage is a message of hope and restoration during difficult times. It speaks to the idea that God will provide abundantly for His people and that they will never again be put to shame. This is a promise of restoration and redemption, even during struggles and hardships.

The passage also speaks to the idea that the Holy Spirit will be poured out on all people, providing them with visions and dreams that will guide them and offer them hope. This suggests that even amid difficult circumstances, God is present and actively at work, providing guidance and comfort to those who seek him.

Joel 2:26-28 is a message of hope and restoration during difficult times, reminding us that God is present and active, even in the darkest moments of our lives. Jeremiah 30:17 speaks of restoration from the storms of life this way; *"For I will restore health to you, and your wounds I will heal, declares the Lord, because they have called you an outcast: 'It is Zion, for whom no one cares!'"*

This verse is part of a larger passage in which God speaks to Prophet Jeremiah about the restoration of Israel after a time of great suffering and exile. The verse is a promise of God's healing power and care for His people, even amid their pain and rejection.

---

*God is present and active, even in*
*the darkest moments of our lives.*

---

When you are experiencing storms in your life, this verse can be a source of comfort and hope, reminding you that God is always with you, even in your darkest moments, and that He has the power to heal your wounds and restore you to health. It also reminds us of God's love and compassion for those who are lonely and forgotten, assuring them that we are never truly alone and that He cares deeply for us.

2 Kings 8:6 describes the restoration of a woman's life after a time of great suffering. *"When the king asked the woman about it, she told him. Then he assigned an official to her case and said to him, 'Give back everything that belonged to her, including all the income from her land from the day she left the country until now."*

The above Scripture is part of a larger story in which the Prophet Elisha raises a woman's son from the dead and helps her recover her property and income lost during a seven-year famine.

The verse is a testament to God's faithfulness and provision for His people, even in difficult circumstances. For those experiencing storms in their lives, this verse can be a source of hope and encouragement. It reminds us that God can restore what has been lost and is always working behind the scenes to bring about our good.

It also reminds us that God's restoration may come through unexpected means, such as the help of a king or an official, and that we should be open to receiving help from others as we navigate our storms.

Restoration after the storms of life can be a challenging and prolonged process, but it is vital for our healing and growth. Below are some steps that can help in the restoration process:

### 1. Allow Yourself To Grieve

It's normal to feel a sense of loss after going through a storm in life. Whether losing a loved one, a job, or something else, it is important to allow yourself to grieve to let out your emotions rather than bottle them up.

### 2. Seek support

Surround yourself with people who care about you and can offer emotional support. This can include family, friends, or a therapist.

### 3. Practice Self-Care

Take care of your physical and emotional needs by eating well, exercising, and engaging in activities that bring you joy and relaxation.

### 4. Focus On The Present

Instead of dwelling in the past or worrying about the future, try to focus on the present moment.

### 5. Set Goals

Set achievable goals for yourself to help you move forward. This can help you feel a sense of purpose and accomplishment.

### 6. Embrace Change

It's natural to resist change, but it's important to embrace it as a part of the restoration process. This can mean trying new things or changing your routine or environment.

Remember, the restoration process is unique to each individual and circumstance and may take time. Be patient and kind to yourself as you work towards healing and growth. For instance, Job 42:10 speaks of Job's restoration after a great storm in his life. *"And the LORD restored Job's losses when he prayed for his friends. Indeed, the LORD gave Job twice as much as he had before."*

---

**Be patient with and kind to yourself, as you work towards healing and growth.**

---

The above verse highlights the importance of prayer and forgiveness in the restoration process. Job's losses were restored when he prayed for his friends and forgave them for their accusations against him. This act of forgiveness and prayer led to his restoration, and he was blessed with twice as much wealth and prosperity as he had before.

From the above verse, we can learn the importance of seeking God during difficult times and relying on Him for restoration and healing. We can also learn the importance of forgiveness and the positive impact it can have on our lives and relationships.

Job's restoration after the storm of life reminds us that there is hope and healing after difficult times and that God can bring blessings and restoration beyond what we can imagine.

Jeremiah 29:10-11 speaks of restoration and hope for the future this way; *"For thus says the LORD: After seventy years are completed at Babylon, I will visit you and perform My good Word toward you and cause you to return to this place. For I know the thoughts that I think toward you says the LORD, thoughts of peace and not of evil, to give you a future and a hope.*

These verses were written to the Israelites who were exiled to Babylon. They were suffering greatly at this time and were probably in a state of despair, but God promised to restore them and give them a future and a hope.

From this passage, we learn that restoration and hope are possible even in the midst of difficult circumstances. God has a plan for our lives, and even when we cannot see it, He is working behind the scenes to bring about our restoration and healing. We can trust in His promises and have faith that He will bring us through the storms of life.

Psalm 51:12 says, *"Restore to me the joy of your salvation and grant me a willing spirit, to sustain me."* This is the psalmist's cry for help from God. This is David seeking restoration and renewal from God. The context of this verse is David's confession and repentance after he committed adultery with Bathsheba and had her husband, Uriah, killed in battle.

Psalm 51 is David's acknowledgment of his sin and asking for God's forgiveness and mercy. He also expresses his desire for a renewed relationship with God and a restored sense of joy and purpose in life.

The phrase "storms of life" is not specifically mentioned in Psalm 51:12. Still, it is a common metaphor used to describe the difficulties and challenges we face daily in this world.

Whether dealing with personal struggles, external circumstances, or a combination of both, we can turn to God for restoration and renewal. As the psalmist says, we can ask God to restore the joy of His salvation and grant us a willing spirit to sustain us through the storms of life.

I Peter 5:10 affirms, *"And the God of all grace, who called you to his eternal glory in Christ, after you have suffered a little while, will himself restore you and make you strong, firm and steadfast."*

This verse speaks to the idea of restoration after suffering. It acknowledges that as believers in Christ, we may experience trials and difficulties in life, but our ultimate hope is in God's eternal glory. The verse also assures that God will restore us, making us strong, firm, and steadfast. This restoration is not just a physical or emotional healing but also a spiritual renewal that strengthens our faith and trust in God.

---

*God has a plan for our lives, and even when we cannot see it, He is working behind the scenes to bring about our restoration and healing.*

---

It can be easy to lose sight of God's goodness and faithfulness while experiencing the storms of life. But this verse reminds us that even amid suffering, we can hold on to the hope of restoration and renewal in Christ.

Also, by placing our trust in God and relying on His grace, we can find the strength to endure and overcome the storms of life.

2 Kings 8:6 says, *"And when the king asked the woman, she told him. So, the king appointed unto her a certain officer, saying,*

*restore all that was hers, and all the fruits of the field since the day that she left the land, even until now."*

This verse is part of the story in which the prophet Elisha helps a woman who had previously been helped by him. The woman's son had died, but Elisha prayed for him, bringing him back to life. Later, when there was a famine in the land, Elisha told the woman to leave and go to another place to live.

However, her property had been taken over by others during her absence. When the woman returned to the land, she went to the king to ask for their restoration. The king asked the woman to tell him her story, and after hearing it, he appointed an officer to restore all that was hers and all the produce from her land since the day she left.

This story speaks to the idea of restoration after a loss or hardship. Even when we face difficult circumstances, we can trust in God's provision and care for us. Like the woman in this story, we can have faith that God will restore what has been taken from us and provide for our needs.

In the storms of life, it can be easy to feel overwhelmed and discouraged. But this story reminds us that God can bring restoration and renewal, even during difficult circumstances. We can trust His faithfulness and provision, knowing He will never leave or forsake us.

---

***You can trust God's faithfulness and provision,***
***knowing He will never leave or forsake you.***

---

PAYE V. BAGNON

# Chapter 9

# Whispers Of Comfort

### The Holy Spirit's Guidance and Comfort In The Midst Of Life's Storms

Are you going through a severe test? Maybe you have lost your appetite, or you haven't slept well for weeks or even months. Fear and panic have replaced quietness and peace. Perhaps you experience loneliness, discouragement, and isolation, complicated by unending physical or emotional pain. You've prayed and asked others to pray for you, and still, there is no relief.

In times of difficulty and hardship, the Holy Spirit can bring comfort and peace to believers through His presence and guidance. The Bible describes the Holy Spirit as a "Helper" who comes through for believers to provide strength and support during challenging times.

John 14:16-17 says, *"And I will ask the Father, and he will give you another advocate to help you and be with you forever the Spirit of truth. The world cannot accept him because it neither sees him nor knows him. But you know him, for he lives with you and will be[a] in you."*

The Holy Spirit plays an important role in helping believers navigate through life's storms. For Christians know that the Holy Spirit is the third person of the Trinity, along with God the Father and Jesus Christ the Son, and that He is sent to guide, comfort, and empower believers in their daily lives.

The Holy Spirit gives believers wisdom and discernment to make wise decisions and navigate difficult situations. Through Him, we are empowered with spiritual gifts, such as the gift of prophecy, healing, and speaking in tongues, which can be used to minister to others and provide comfort and encouragement during times of distress.

Ultimately, the Holy Spirit is a source of hope and strength that can help you weather life's storms and come out stronger on the other side. Through prayer and meditation on the Word of God and cultivating a relationship with the Holy Spirit, we will experience His guidance and comfort even amid life's most challenging circumstances.

> *Ultimately, the Holy Spirit is a source of hope and strength that can help you weather life's storms and come out stronger on the other side.*

### Empowerment through the Holy Spirit

The Holy Spirit plays a crucial role in helping us navigate life's storms as He is sent to guide, comfort, and empower believers daily. In times of hardship, the Holy Spirit can bring comfort and peace to believers through His presence and guidance. The Bible describes the Holy Spirit as a "Helper" who comes alongside believers to provide strength and support during challenging times (John 14:16-17).

The Holy Spirit can also give believers wisdom and discernment to make wise decisions and understand mysteries. Additionally, the Holy Spirit is said to empower believers with spiritual gifts, such as the gift of prophecy, healing, and speaking in tongues, which can be used to minister to others and provide comfort and encouragement during times of distress.

Moreover, the Holy Spirit helps us endure trials and tribulations by assuring God's love and faithfulness. The Holy Spirit reminds us that we are not alone, and that God is with us, even amid life's storms.

Ultimately, Christians believe that the Holy Spirit is a source of hope and strength that can help weather life's storms and come out stronger on the other side. We can experience His guidance and comfort through the Holy Spirit, even in the most challenging circumstances.

Romans 8:26 is a powerful verse in the Bible that provides comfort and hope for us in difficult times. *"In the same way, the Spirit helps us in our weakness. We do not know what we ought to pray for, but the Spirit himself intercedes for us through wordless groans."*

This verse reminds us that even when we don't know what to pray for or how to express our deepest needs to God, the Holy Spirit is there to help us. The Holy Spirit intercedes for us with groans too deep for words. This means He communicates our needs to God on our behalf, even when we don't have the words to express them ourselves.

In times of difficulty, we may feel overwhelmed, anxious, or uncertain about the future. We may not know how to pray or what to ask for. But the Holy Spirit is there to help us. He understands our needs and communicates them to God in a way that only He can.

Knowing that the Holy Spirit is interceding for us can bring comfort and peace in difficult times. It reminds us that we are not alone, and that God is with us, even in the midst of our struggles.

*Even when we don't know what to pray for or how to express our deepest needs to God, the Holy Spirit is there to help us.*

### Comfort, Strength, and Guidance Through the Holy Spirit

As we rely on the Holy Spirit's guidance and comfort, we can trust that God is working all things together for our good and that He has a plan and purpose for our lives, even during life's challenges. *"And we know that in all things God works for the good of those who love him, who have been called according to his purpose"* (Romans 8:28).

In 2 Corinthians 4:8-9, the Apostle Paul wrote about the trials and tribulations he and his fellow believers endured in their ministry. *"We are hard pressed on every side, but not crushed; perplexed, but not in despair; persecuted, but not abandoned; struck down, but not destroyed."*

In this context, the role of the Holy Spirit is to provide comfort, strength, and guidance to us amid life's storms. The Holy Spirit is often referred to as the Comforter or the Counselor. Paul's words in 2 Corinthians suggest that believers can endure the hardships that come their way through the power of the Holy Spirit.

The Holy Spirit is also the source of spiritual gifts and abilities that enable believers to serve God and others in the face of adversity.

These gifts include wisdom, discernment, faith, and perseverance, among other gifts, which are essential for weathering life's storms.

Ultimately, the role of the Holy Spirit in our lives is to lead us into a deeper relationship with God and to empower us to live out our faith in a way that brings glory to Him, even during difficult circumstances.

*"For I am convinced that neither death nor life, neither angels nor demons, neither the present nor the future, nor any powers, neither height nor depth, nor anything else in all creation, will be able to separate us from the love of God that is in Christ Jesus our Lord"* (Romans 8:38-39).

In this passage, the role of the Holy Spirit in life's storms is to provide assurance and confidence to us that nothing can separate us from the love of God. The Holy Spirit testifies to our spirit that we are children of God and have been adopted into His family through faith in Jesus Christ.

Therefore, even during trials and tribulations, we can have peace and hope, knowing that we are secure in God's love and that nothing can separate us from it. The Holy Spirit also intercedes for believers in prayer, helping us communicate with God when we may not have the words or are too overwhelmed to express ourselves. The Spirit helps us to pray according to God's will and to trust that He is working all things together for our good, even amid difficult circumstances.

Overall, the Holy Spirit plays a crucial role during the storms of our lives by providing assurance, peace, hope, and intercession. Through the power of the Holy Spirit, we can persevere and overcome any challenge, knowing that God is with us and His love will never fail us.

### David's Confidence in God's Deliverance

Psalm 3 is a prayer of David in a time of distress, when he was fleeing from his own son Absalom who had staged a rebellion against him. In this psalm, David expresses his confidence in God's protection and deliverance amid his troubles.

*"LORD, how many are my foes! How many rise up against me! Many are saying of me, "God will not deliver him." But you, LORD, are a shield around me, my glory, the One who lifts my head high. I call out to the LORD, and he answers me from his holy mountain. I lie down and sleep; I wake again because the LORD sustains me. I will not fear though tens of thousands assail me on every side. Arise, LORD! Deliver me, my God! Strike all my enemies on the jaw; break the teeth of the wicked. From the LORD comes deliverance. May your blessing be on your people."*

The role of the Holy Spirit in life's storms, as seen in Psalm 3, is to provide strength, comfort, and guidance to believers in times of adversity. David acknowledges that it is the Lord who sustains him and lifts his head, even when he is surrounded by enemies. This implies that the Holy Spirit gives believers the courage and hope to face their challenges and keep their faith in God, even when everything seems to be against them.

David also recognizes that salvation belongs to the Lord and that He is a shield around His people. The Holy Spirit helps us to understand that our ultimate salvation is in God's hands and that nothing can separate us from His love and protection. This can give us the confidence to face life's storms with faith and trust in God, knowing He will never abandon us.

Finally, David ends the psalm with a prayer for God to bless His people. The Holy Spirit helps us focus on God's blessings and look beyond our present circumstances, knowing He has good plans for us. Just like David reached out to God for help in his darkest hour, ask the Holy Spirit for comfort, help, and guidance in your distress.

Through the Holy Spirit, you can find peace during life's storms, trusting that God is working all things together for your good.

PAYE V. BAGNON

# About The Author

Rev. Paye V. Bagnon is a pastor and motivational speaker whose global ministry has transformed many people's lives worldwide. His practical, inspired teachings have greatly blessed people from all walks of life. He received the mandate to start Faith Life Ministries International in Paynesville, Monrovia, Liberia, West Africa, where he serves as the Founder and General Overseer, with churches in Liberia and USA.

Rev. Paye V. Bagnon is recognized as a visionary leader with an apostolic, prophetic, teaching, and evangelistic anointing. He was married to Rev. Mother Cynthia MB Bagnon, who is deceased, and their marriage is blessed with two beautiful children.

**Paye V. Bagnon**
**Faith Life Books**
**Moses Biah Road**
**Paynesville City**
**Monrovia, Liberia,**
**P. O Box 2129**
**+2318863523943**

**Email:** faithlifebook74@gmail.com

Made in the USA
Coppell, TX
08 October 2023

22572569R00059